war / torn

poems by

Peter Vanderberg

Finishing Line Press
Georgetown, Kentucky

war / torn

ACKNOWLEDGMENTS

I would like to thank Dr. Steven Alvarez at St. John's University, under whose
guidance these poems were written, and my classmates at St. John's who gave
me the suggestions and confidence to make this chapbook.
I would also like to thank the editors at *Pleiades* who first published "I am as
much to blame as anyone—" in the spring of 2023.

Publisher: Leah Huete de Maines
Editor: Christen Kincaid
Cover Art: James Vanderberg
Author Photo: Peter Vanderberg
Cover Design: Elizabeth Maines McCleavy

Order online: www.finishinglinepress.com
also available on amazon.com

Author inquiries and mail orders:
Finishing Line Press
PO Box 1626
Georgetown, Kentucky 40324
USA

Table of Contents

When will the war begin?

    Maybe it already has. News
is delayed—event ignites, shreds cars, crumbles concrete—
      we are first to die.
      You will never hear our true stories.

    For us it was a blank war,
just a bad day bound to everyone
      else's bad days coming. Then reports

      emerge: black smoke billowing
over horizon—who fired mortars & why?
      How many sons died in mud & snow?

      How many dragged from the wreckage
of their lives into new cinder lives
      suspended between prayer & morphine?

News must reach a safer place

        where fragments

    stitch into senseless sentences.

Where unnecessary details (names, last words,
        whose bullets burrowed into their hearts,

what questions troubled their sky) can be cut

        like fat on the butcher's block.

Still, I would not know the war had begun.

        My room is too quiet.

Dog running in her sleep

                                   distant sound of workers
                  repaving our street (layers of broken road reveal

black lines written
in the accidental script of tragedy—

                        we are free to bury memory)

                                           at the agreed upon pace

              while workers watch workers

              take turns
              slowly   carefully

              assembling
              the day's lunch order.

They talk about the war in Ukraine.

        They know who to blame.

Only when it gets so quiet that I can hear

my own pulse & even the dog's troubled dreams
    hunting cardinals & starlings of extraordinary color
    have calmed

        Only then will I open *The Times* online
        & face news that war

    nameless and confused
        has not begun

    it always was
        beginning

        & the people in Kyiv

    never pronounce their home
    as I've always done

    Split my oppressor's tongue

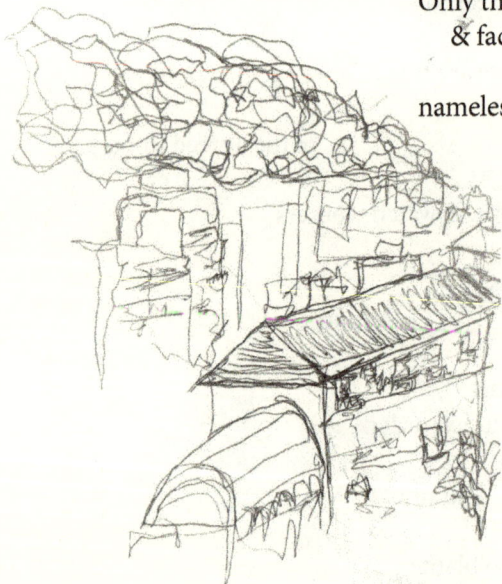

Young refugees watch

a man between empire-red flags

speaking through   hotel TV

Their child plays with plastic soldiers

on the snowy landscape   of bed sheets

A few soldiers   have already fallen

They are the same soldiers   my sons

play war with   in the trenches   of our backyard

I taught them to cover   their wounded

with thatched twigs   grass & leaves

so to avoid   enemy planes

bombs come at night   or just before dawn

fire-&-forget missiles erase our memory

& do not follow the rules

My daughter reads my fortune in loose tea leaves.

Our grandmother's cup & saucer offer painted symbols—
open hand with open eye in the palm,
ship at sail, bleeding heart, open birdcage—
signs of what waits.

My mother had given this to her mother
who, one day after coffee in her kitchen, gave it to me.

Today I passed the cup
to Sara & she made darjeeling tea.
After swirling leaves the cup reveals
what I already knew—

tragedy rings every rim your lips press.
Some work still to be done & love,
it seems, might come true for some.

Tanks grind toward Ukraine,

our house trembles. Noel growls,
mohawk raised down her back. We watch
a dozer roll down our street loaded
with stones as if the enemy
come to bury us under the ruble
of our own homes

and not someone's father just doing his job.

I don't think I could shoot a man
who wasn't looking at me unless
he was looking for my children,
then, perhaps, wound with intent to ruin.

Load new posts

I am as much to blame as anyone—

sitting here smoking under silver maple buds,
mistranslating the language of birds.

I laugh & play war with my children,
praise their drawings of tanks & warplanes,
tell stories about when I lived on a warship.

> After the captain went to sleep
> we searched for satellites among stars
> with military-grade binoculars.

> Between Venus & our beloved moon
> a red pulse drifting through night reminded us
> that someone is listening.

I don't tell my boys about watching explosions
on the horizon, or the weight of loading live rounds.

Everyone prays in their own language,

trying not to pray for things they don't deserve
like winning the lotto, or having to bury their children,
or to be perfectly happy, sitting in the sun,

while others bury their children,
or to be inexplicably happy while others
are praying for the chance just to bury their children.

We pray for God to leave us alone—
to never rattle our walls, to keep wars
at a safe distance. Every prayer
is answered, or already has been,

or will be, though we may not know
that the cause for prayer waits
in the tragedies of our inheritance.

Beloved:

your life will be

      smoke that appears   disappears

Blessed are those who   pay

      ransom to God

the Kingdom of Heaven is theirs

        way & truth & life

whoever is not against us   is for us

      Keep salt within yourselves
        and you will have peace
      with one another.

The poet speaks

through video call
    we watch from our poorly-lit rooms

    throw questions to the chat box

    sing praise before poems end

Close reading

comes from a tradition of sacred reading

my father would hold a book
he would read to us in prayer-voice

we didn't know any better

golden ratio

of words to quantum of meaning

He reads, *The kingdom of heaven is good.*

But heaven on earth is better.

We contemplate ratios:

real / surreal

*

seen / unseen

*

lover / beloved

*

war / peace

Please,

tell us about the ratio between prayer & poetry.

Tell us that seeing   is perceiving

                                                      is witness,

& that writing   is preserving

                                                      is prayer.

Tell us that there was once a time of

                                        no war.

It troubles me

I am trying to understand the presence of

        there are problems I have been trying to solve my whole life

        I think my father gave them to me

Last question:

What is the role of the poet during times of war?

Answer:

run.

We wake slowly, drink coffee, choose a gospel

to carry through the day. In another time zone

they wake to nightmare, drink tap water,
choose what to save from the fire.

Prayers pour from wet trenches, are poured
into sandbags, fall from the sky as snow or ash.

I will not fly to Poland, walk across the border,
take a rifle & wait to kill another man.

I will protect myself, scroll news, die a slow,
comfortable death softened by nurses & morphine.

Front page news—family of four laying in the street,
one girl is eight years old. My eight year old asks—

. . .

They are sleeping, I say. They must be so tired.
The soldiers are trying to wake them.

dry leaves

blowing

leaves

                                        cross the road

rest on the girl's red coat

                            in her gold hair

                        one

caught in her open hand

In my country,

men go on adventures.
The best of these end in war.

They thank me
for my service
every chance they get.

Everything
I eat or burn
comes from a place

I call
war / torn
but have never touched.

A family leaves broken

windows & molotov cocktails behind—
belongings stuffed in backpacks & plastic grocery bags.
Car idling, the driver looks at his phone.
An older woman, last to leave their house,
leans on her cane, waiting for a sign.

She could be your grandmother.

Soldiers, let
     down your guard
          let grandmother ghosts come

       between you

    & every inbound live round.

          Let babus' have their way,

             amen.

Peter Vanderberg is the author of *Crossing Pleasant Lake* (Red Bird Chapbooks), *celestial navigation* (Finishing Line Press), and *Drownproof* (Black Centipede Press). His poems have appeared in journals such as *Prairie Schooner, Drunken Boat, Lumina,* and *Cura.* He is the Founding Editor of Ghostbird Press, publishing chapbooks since 2011. After serving in the U.S. Navy from 1999 -2003, he received an MFA in Creative Writing from Queens College, City University of New York. Peter teaches English and writing at Chaminade High School and is currently a Ph.D candidate at St. John's University.

www.ingramcontent.com/pod-product-compliance
Lightning Source LLC
Chambersburg PA
CBHW022109080426
42734CB00009B/1533